Seashore Birds

by Peter Gill

illustrated by the author

Published by Dinosaur Publications

The coast, where the land meets the sea,
attracts many kinds of birds.
Some birds live on salt marshes and
estuaries. Some nest and find food
on cliffs and beaches. Others spend
most of their life at sea and
come to the coast only to nest.

Birds on migration rest and feed on
the coast during their long flights.

Anyone visiting the seaside sees and
hears the noisy, quarrelsome gulls.
The **Herring Gull** is the most common
It feeds on almost anything – refuse
and fish waste as well as other
birds' eggs and chicks.

At nesting time, the male and female Herring Gulls choose a nest site on his territory. When the eggs hatch, the chicks peck at the red spot on their parents' beaks, begging for food. Young gulls have brownish plumage for two years.

The **Common Gull** is
smaller than the
Herring Gull, but not so common.

The **Black-headed Gull** nests
in colonies on salt marshes.
In winter, it loses its
black 'cap' head feathers.

In the breeding season, the
Great Black-backed Gull eats
young birds and rabbits.
It chases other gulls
and steals their food.

The **Kittiwake** spends most of its time at sea.

Manx Shearwaters live at sea. At night, they visit their nests in burrows on islands.

The **Fulmar** lives over the ocean gliding on every up-current of air. It nests on cliff faces and sometimes on buildings.

Gannets make spectacular dives
for fish near their great nesting colonies.
When the young leave the nest, they
weigh more than their parents.

Cormorants often rest with their wings outstretched to dry their feathers, which are not water-proof like ducks' feathers.

Shags are smaller than Cormorants and have crests at nesting time. Both swim under water to catch fish.

The **Puffin** has only one nestling and can carry many sprats and sand-eels in its large beak to feed it.

The **Guillemot's** egg is very pointed so that it rolls in a circle and not off the ledge.

The **Razorbill** nests among rocks or in small caves.

Arctic Skua

Great Skua

The **Skua** gets food by chasing
other sea birds to make them
drop their catch.
It eats other birds and
their eggs too.

Sandwich Tern

Arctic Tern

Terns, with their slender wings and forked tails, are often called 'sea-swallows'. They nest on open beaches and dunes and their eggs and chicks are hard to see against the sand and pebbles. Terns swoop on people to protect their chicks.

Common Tern

They migrate to the southern oceans
to spend the winter. The Arctic Tern
even flies to the Antarctic.

Little Tern

Many kinds of long-legged waders feed
along the shore. Their beaks are of
different lengths and shapes so that
they can feed on the small creatures
living on the water, sand and mud
or below the surface.

The black and white **Oystercatcher**
often looks as if it is asleep but
it noisily warns other birds of danger.
It prises open cockles and mussels
with its strong bill.

The **Redshank** uses its long beak
to probe for small crabs and
shrimps burrowing in the mud.

The **Curlew** has the longest bill
of all the waders to reach
ragworms deep in the mud.

The **Whimbrel** is like
a small Curlew
with a shorter beak
and striped head.

The **Avocet** sweeps its
curving bill from side to side,
taking tiny creatures from
the surface of the water.

Two kinds of Godwit feed on coastal
mud flats. **The Bar-tailed Godwit**
prefers to feed above the tideline.
The **Black-tailed Godwit** often wades
deep in the water and soft mud.

The **Common Sandpiper**
makes jerky, restless
movements and
bobs its tail.

The **Ringed Plover's** nest and eggs
are well camouflaged and are often
trodden on. The birds try to lead
people away by pretending to have
a broken wing.

Great flocks of **Knots** change like magic from white to dark as they twist and turn.

The **Dunlins,** the most common of waders, are quick, busy feeders.

Summer

Winter

The **Turnstone** got its name because it feeds by turning over stones to catch sand hoppers.
Migrant **Sanderlings** from the Arctic feed busily like clockwork toys before flying on.

Turnstone

Sanderling

In olden days, people thought migrant **Barnacle Geese** had hatched out of Goose Barnacle shells, which are found on the shore.

Brent Geese feed in winter on eel-grass growing on tidal mud flats.

Pink-footed Geese feed on stubble in fields close to the coast. When the moon is bright, they feed all night too.

Shelducks nest in old rabbit burrows or in other holes.

Pintails feed and roost on estuaries in the winter.

Wigeon have strong short bills to cut and pull the grasses and sea weeds they eat.

Long-tailed ducks dive for food in shallow sea near the coast.

Eider ducks have soft down, which people collect from their nests for quilts and pillows.

In winter, **Common Scoters** often fly in long lines along the coast.

The **Peregrine Falcon** glides high in the sky then makes its spectacular stoop, diving with wings half closed on a fleeing bird.

Choughs play in the up-currents
of air near the cliff faces
where they nest.
They eat ants and grubs
from the cliff-top turf.

Many **Jackdaws** nest on rocky cliffs.
They sometimes perch on
a sheep's back and pull out
the wool to line their nests.

Rock Doves, ancestors of
town pigeons, are only found
on the wildest coasts.

The **Rock Pipit** nests in a crevice
and sings as it flies up from
the rocks and glides down again.

In winter, small flocks of
Snow Buntings feed on the seeds
of plants growing in the shingle.

In bad weather, strong winds
blow migrant birds to the coast
from faraway countries.

Alpine Swift

Bluethroat

Hoopoe

Text and illustrations copyright © Peter Gill 1986

Published by Dinosaur Publications
8 Grafton Street
London W1X 3LA

Dinosaur Publications is an imprint
of the Children's Division, part of
the Collins Publishing Group

Printed by Warners of Bourne and London